remembering joy

An inspiring collection of contributions
for everyone to enjoy
from service users and staff of
The Leonard Cheshire
Randall Close Centre in London

Compiled and edited by
Audrey Burns Ross and Elizabeth Ann Stuart

This book is dedicated to The Leonard Cheshire family
worldwide, and to the memory of its Founder, Group
Captain Lord Cheshire V.C., O.M., D.S.O., D.F.C.,
who founded the Charity in the aftermath of the Second
World War. Today, it is the leading charity provider of
care and support for disabled people in the U.K.
and overseas.

A Leonard Cheshire Foundation Imprint

ISBN 0-9512471-6- 6

British Library Cataloguing - in - Publication Data.
A catalogue record for this book is available from the British Library.

Designed, printed and bound in Great Britain by Prontaprint Fulham, London SW6.

remembering joy

It is a great privilege to write the foreword to this stimulating collection of remembrances and expressions of joy from so many different personal viewpoints.

The collection contains many very thought provoking views of life and poignant vignettes. It is the sort of book that one feels better for having read, and puts down with a smile on one's face. I heartily commend it to all potential readers. It will cause each to draw breath and consider their own joyous memories.

I would like to offer my warmest congratulations to all those involved with the production, those who compiled and edited the collection and, above all, the contributors - the clients and staff at Randall Close Leonard Cheshire Centre.

Bryan Dutton
Director General
Leonard Cheshire

Creating opportunities with disabled people

LEONARD CHESHIRE

The Origins and Story of The Leonard Cheshire Red Feather Emblem

Leonard Cheshire's red feather logo dates back to the late 1950s in Singapore.

The local Leonard Cheshire services were planning a fundraising flag day, and wanted to use something a little different from the usual paper flags - something which would make people sit up and take notice. It was a volunteer with the residential service in Singapore who suggested using a feather instead. They decided to dye the feathers red, both to symbolise courage, and because in parts of South East Asia the colour stands for happiness and prosperity.

The idea worked, and soon spread out to other Leonard Cheshire projects. Before long, the red feather logo was being used worldwide wherever the Leonard Cheshire name was known.

It was not until four decades later, in the early 1990s, that the organisation decided to standardise the design of the logo, by which time there were well over one hundred different versions in use! The current logo was adopted during 1998, the Golden Jubilee Year.

Any proceeds from the sale of
"Remembering Joy" will be put towards the
provision and maintenance of a sensory
garden at Randall Close, thereby providing
an additional strand of joy for current and
future service users.

William J. Gallagher
Service Manager

INTRODUCTION

joy is something which oozes from every pore. It can be seen from the eyes, heard in the voice, is apparent in movement, and shines from the individual like a beacon of light.

What an amazingly joyful experience this has been! How could we ever have envisaged the end result of this idea?

We sincerely hope that the insights and treasures which have unfolded in this book will bring you as much joy and enlightenment as we have experienced during its compilation.

Each of us comes in to this world as a unique divine spark but, in the noisy confusion of life, particularly if one is disabled, finding a platform where one can be heard is not always easy.

This book is a platform!

ABR & EAS.

ACKNOWLEDGEMENTS

This inspiring book exists because of the deep commitment by many people, and we are indebted to all those who have taken time to share personal reflections on joy. The book is testament to their insight, wisdom, humour, and love of life.

That so many service users and Randall Close staff have been so enthusiastic about the project has made the past year such a joy for us.

We should also like to thank the Director General of The Leonard Cheshire Foundation, Bryan Dutton, for his foreword and general enthusiasm for the project.

Our thanks also go to Rosemarie Mitchell, the Regional Director, for her general help and for writing such a lovely poem.

Special thanks are due to William J. Gallagher, the Service Manager at Randall Close, who has been unstinting in his support and encouragement from the moment this idea was suggested to him.

Gratitude is also due to our printers, Gerry Torosyan and Nesli Hollinshead, for their tremendous patience and artistic expertise, so necessary in the publishing of this book.

Audrey Burns Ross would like to express her personal thanks to Elizabeth Haylett at The Society of Authors for all her help on copyright law, moral rights, permissions and self publishing. Her guidance in these matters has been invaluable during the final administrations.

We thank them all for understanding what we have been trying to do, and why!

ABR & EAS.

CONTENTS

LIST OF CONTRIBUTORS IN ALPHABETICAL ORDER

The contributors on this list are all disabled adults with the exception of a few Leonard Cheshire staff who were invited to contribute and are indicated by an asterisk.

We remember with deep affection the contributors who sadly passed away during the compilation of this book. Their contributions are listed with the others in order of receipt.

Should you wish to access a specific piece, please refer to the alphabetical list at the front with appropriate pages.

Contributions, where people have preferred to remain anonymous, appear at intermittent intervals throughout the anthology.

Leonard Cheshire

Sybil Carter-Allen

I remember vividly the day I was
baptised. I was about 18 - 20 years
old. I felt so good and remember it
as if it were yesterday. I will
always remember it.
I remember feeling that God
was guiding me to come to
the United Kingdom.
There was some reason why
God wanted me to come.
Perhaps it was that I could set a
good example because, at that
time in the sixties, the black and
white communities were rather suspicious of each other.
Inspired by my feelings at my baptism, I found the
strength to do my best for my community.

I still feel like this today.

1

Waverney Lewis

I get great joy from cooking meals
and baking cakes. At home, we
always did a lot of cooking and
creating our own recipes.
In Guyana we eat a lot of rice,
plantain, yam, sweet potatoes
and edo. We also use
salt fish. When the fish is
cooked we cut it up and give
everyone a piece and they eat it
with a fry of sweet pepper and onion.

My joy is seeing people enjoying my concoctions.

I am passionate about good food.

Leonard Cheshire

Writer Anon.

I was going through a very bad patch
and, at that time, I was thinking about
whom I would meet when my time
came up. I was thinking about
members of my family and my
friends. As I was going through,
and thinking whom I would
meet first, I heard this voice
boom out saying, "I have not
given up on you!" My spirits lifted immediately and I
knew that God was still there. I felt completely at peace
with myself knowing that God was taking care of me.

Now, I can think of that incident whenever I feel low,
and my spirits feel immediately uplifted.

Leonard Cheshire

Edwin Yearwood

I love music. My soul is uplifted

when I listen to my favourite pieces.

My favourites are:-

1) Elizabethan Serenade.

2) Blue Danube Waltz.

3) Anything by Fred Astaire.

I loved dancing to Fred Astaire's music when I was

young. Now I listen and enjoy it.

4

Leonard Cheshire

Elizabeth Grant

I love listening to music which

makes me feel good. I feel it

in my body, turn up the

volume, and dance.

All kinds of music

move my body and

I feel on top of the world.

Leonard Cheshire

Joyce Nelson

I love music and dancing. I like

reggae, religious music, calypso,

and in fact my tastes in

music are very eclectic.

I love it all.

On days when I feel low

I turn on jazz or calypso

(I love Louis Armstrong)

and I am soon lifted

into another world.

Sometimes, I imagine I am taking off on concorde. I am

sitting there imagining the sensation and I feel great !

Leonard Cheshire
Joyce Nelson

I still remember our (a group from

Randall Close) visit

to the bluebell woods.

I sat there enjoying

the pleasure and

scenery of it all.

I felt I was sitting

in a heavenly place.

I still visualise that scene when we were all there and my

spirits are immediately uplifted.

Leonard Cheshire

Pearl Nicholas

Music and dance

seem like the

same thing

to me.

I love

them both.

I love the

rhythm.

Leonard Cheshire
ARTURA

SPECIAL MOMENTS

My most special moment and
place is in the countryside, when
the thunder is rolling in the
distance, the clouds are grey,
and the weather is warm.
To me this is a very magical
time, and I find that my
energy is replenished so
that I may meet all that
life can aim at me.
I am then renewed.

My other time that makes me feel good is when I am at
Festivals and we are drumming. The sound of many
drums all playing together brings out a powerful energy
that can be tapped into by all who are present.

Leonard Cheshire

John Azzopardi

I get great joy from watching

football, darts, tennis,

running. In fact, I love

all sport. Sometimes

I go to a live Chelsea

match. My favourite

Italian team is Roma.

Leonard Cheshire

Phyllis Green

I feel really happy when

I come to Randall Close,

especially on a Friday,

when I do flower

arrangements which

I love. I also feel

very happy because

I can be with my

friends there. My

friends help me on my

way and I can share

important things with

them.

Trust is very important in life.

Leonard Cheshire
Pauline Marshall

The glow of excitement

(and contentment) of

my 'group' winning

so many of the

entries in the

Garden and

Flower Show -

2 firsts, 3 seconds

and one third.

I felt as if I had

won the lottery!!

Leonard Cheshire

Writer Anon.

Being inspired

by a fabulous

poem which

really spoke

to me.

Terry Whittaker

In April 1996 I went to the Wolfson Medical Centre. There, I had my first contact with a deck of Tarot cards, when I met Artura (Arthur West). Four years ago I was told by a medium that I had the gift for reading the Tarot. In May 2001 I attended a talk on the Tarot at a Psychic Fair. I found out that the lady was a teacher of the Tarot and I knew that she was the person to teach me.

So, in September 2001, I attended evening classes and passed my exam (with distinction) on 12th January 2002.

I was surprised how much I learnt about myself. The cards got me to open up, whereas no person has ever done this.

Now, I have started doing readings at Psychic and Health Fairs. I get so much satisfaction, knowing that I have been able to help and advise others.

I have all my confidence back. It is a great way to meet people. Also, I have noticed that when I am in that environment all my pain goes. I forget all my own problems.

I have made 78 new loyal friends (78 Tarot Cards). No doubt I will make lots more contacts and NEW FRIENDS.

REMEMBER, you don't know what you can do until you try!

My happiest times have been spent on holiday in Austria. I feel more at home there than I do here. My spiritual home.

Leonard Cheshire

Denise Mich - Onyibe

Since Leonard Cheshire took over Randall Close I have felt like a human being. I feel my eyes were not open before, but now they are. I am seeing life more clearly. I have a voice. They listen to me. I feel happy, have greater peace of mind, and look forward to coming here. The Centre gives me confidence. Before, I was quieter. Now, I speak up for myself and am not afraid anymore. My awareness of life has deepened and I do not get so anxious and tense.

I feel a personal unfolding at the moment and, to be honest, I just feel free and enjoy life more. I feel excited which is a new experience for me.

I look forward to the future here.

Leonard Cheshire
Bernie-Rose Rehal

I call Randall Close my home and I get great joy from coming here.

When I first started I was afraid of disability, but after getting to know everyone as individuals, I got on great with them, and still do. I'd love to be able to do more for everyone!

At first, after my accident, I found it hard, and I thought no-one would want to speak to me. I kept a barrier round me. I had to regain joy because I had lost everything, my friends and family. I didn't want my family to worry.

Now, I've gained another family and I love it! My confidence is coming back.

I love to make other clients laugh. That is a joy to me. That way I am covering up my own pain.

I hope people do not think I am loud. I want to be accepted by everyone. I have no self esteem. What comes out is not always what I want. With the other service users it is different. However, I do feel more confident.

cont'd.

Leonard Cheshire

The Day Centre has taught me such a lot and I do feel better.

My first priority now is my life. My life was on hold. I'd like to do more to help here. It gives me such joy to do it.

Away from Randall Close my joy is my Yorkie, Toby. I love him to bits!

Another joy I have is my garden. It is my passion! I got the inspiration from Pauline Bushell's (another service user) garden. I get great relief just looking at it. So that I can look at it more I have changed my bedroom and living room around. Most of my time I spend on the sofa in my living room just looking at my garden and I feel relaxed.

Leonard Cheshire

Ron Gerrard

There are certain pieces of music

which, when I hear them,

almost force me to stop

and listen because they

are so beautiful. Such a

piece is Bizet's "The Pearl

Fishers." That gives me

great joy.

BRINGS JOY AND HAPPINESS
AND APPRECIATION

1. Birth of my two daughters.
2. When my husband brought me a lovely rose from the garden, which he had grown, and told me how much he loved me.
3. Beautiful sun-set.
4. Field of daffodils.
5. When we had our first grandchild.
6. Knowing the name of our creator (God) Jehovah.
7. Listening to a soothing piece of music and relaxing.
8. Walking on the sand by the sea. (bare feet)
9. Having good friends
10. Appreciating our life in health and sickness.

Leonard Cheshire

Ruby Gormley

I've seen so many paintings by

famous artists and the

cobbled streets where they

sat doing their work.

I love art, and the

pictures I have seen

have taken me miles

and miles away from

everything. It is as if

I am in a different world

at those times.

I can't actually express how I feel about some of

the art I have seen.

Leonard Cheshire
Ruby Gormley

I feel great joy and peace with
myself when I do my deep
breathing and relaxation in
yoga groups. I feel all my
anger and frustrations melt
away. It lets it all out, and
I feel I have found a little
bit of peace in myself.

I enjoy exploring myself
in this way. I want
to go a little bit further
into my mind and
I know all the anger
and frustrations will
gradually go. This, I know,
will in the end help me.

In the group I can trust everyone, and I can let my
feelings go and tell them how I feel. This also helps
me.

It is like a big heavy load exploding away from me,
from my whole being.

Leonard Cheshire
Ruby Gormley

I love the freedom travel

gives me. Seeing new

places and other people

of different cultures

and languages which

I have never explored

before fascinates me.

The scenery, the

beautiful countryside,

and I feel as if I am born

again, and beginning

again.

Florrie Chatting

I get a lovely feeling when

I am doing tapestry and

printing. I have just

done a big tapestry

showing hotels,

chimney pots,

different colours

of sky, and it is going

to be hung in the

Church. I enjoy

doing this.

Leonard Cheshire

Pauline Bushell

I remember the very first holiday I ever had. We went to Ramsgate. I would be about fifteen years old. I was with my parents and my two brothers and my aunt(my mother's sister). I remember the feelings of excitement because we were going away for a whole week instead of the odd day. I couldn't wait, and I can still feel that feeling of joy welling up inside me when I think about it.

Nowadays, the euphoria I felt is not experienced in the same way by teenagers. They expect more out of life than we did, but do they have the same joy? I wonder.

I remember the excitement of the unknown, the joy of family life, and the security of always knowing the family was there.

Now that my life has changed considerably, and I no longer have my parents, nevertheless, inside myself I have the memories of my secure childhood provided by them.

cont'd

Leonard Cheshire

Nowadays, my brothers who live out of London, are always ready to give me a helping hand if I need it, especially the younger one, and my cousin who helps with shopping etc.

It is sad that in the modern world, for one reason or another, families have tended to drift apart which makes me feel sad.

However, I am lucky that some of mine are still around me, including my niece, who lives with me and helps me out. She is like the daughter I never had.

I also have two cats, Toby and Barney, who are part of the family. My niece also has a pet rat called Jasper who is quite tame!

As you can see, family has always been important to me. It is part of who I am. My joy and wellbeing in life comes mainly from my family.

Leonard Cheshire
John Wheeler

Immediately, there comes to
mind the birth of my grand-
daughter, Poppy. Feelings
of pride and joy and
thoughts of what a
wonderful daughter
my son, Jon, and
Alex, have produced.
She is wonderful! What
a miracle birth is! We are
having such a wonderful
time! It is lovely. A new
young life and my wife and
I feel so much better.

Leonard Cheshire

Cynthia Fairbairn

We have a caravan in the heart of the Surrey countryside.
It is in a small wood surrounded by green fields. Just
being there I feel a sense of peace and contentment.

One of the things that gives me great pleasure is to sit
outside on a warm summer evening with a nice cup of
tea, and just experience the beauty of God's Creation.

I watch the birds coming down for a bath before retiring.
The rabbits are in the fields having their evening meal,
and last playtime before bed, one assumes. I marvel at the
antics of the squirrels in the trees playing hide and seek
and catch me if you can.

If I am really quiet, and really lucky, I might see a deer
come by for a drink of water.

As the time goes on, and the wildlife retire, it is good to
sit and watch the sun set, and the kaleidoscope of colour
as nature prepares for yet another day.

Once again I marvel at the abundance of God's diversity
and generosity to the world.

Leonard Cheshire

Writer Anon.

Enjoying a

carpet of

bluebells

on a

beautiful

Spring

morning.

Leonard Cheshire
Blossom Reid

I had a wonderful

feeling going

on holiday

to Jamaica,

getting off the

plane, and seeing

all the beautiful scenery.

THE SHORE AT NIGHT

The waves are breaking o'er the pebbled beach,

The moon is sparkling as night falls,

The stars light up the darkened sky,

A mist lies overall.

From a birds-eye view I survey the scene

Alone, but not lonely, as I sit in a dream, on a beach by the shore.

This is the place I wish to be.

It's so peaceful,

So calm,

So refreshingly cool.

As time passes by a new dawn is awakening.

The sun gently falls to the sea.

It rests, and is still shimmering slightly as a pathway appears,

Shedding a silvery light in it's wake.

Reluctantly now, I make a move, but,

Forever the scene will remain

In the recesses of my mind.

A Poem written by
Joan Hubbert 2002

Leonard Cheshire
Kofi Boateng

I was born in Ghana in 1940. My
earliest childhood memories are of
listening to the brass bands, and
watching the dancers, which
were a major part of Ghanaian
life in those days. They made
everyone feel so happy.

I joined in and played in a
brass band while I lived
in Ghana.

I came to London in 1957 to work, but in all the years I
have been here I have never forgotten the sights and
sounds when the brass bands played and I played in
them.

Leonard Cheshire
Jo Burden

Watching my children around the

garden table at Sunday lunch

chatting, laughing, and teasing

each other, and watching

their children playing in

the garden in the

summertime!

Sitting by the sea watching

the waves on a rugged

coastline with a slight breeze.

Motoring through the mountains and stopping at

the foot of Mt. Blanc, a truly magical sight!!

Leonard Cheshire
Jackie Miller

To me every day is a bonus! You see, they did not think I would survive. They laid me on my mother's stomach, thinking I was stillborn. They were cleaning her up (that is the way she always put it) when she felt me move. She did not even know what she had. They had wrapped me up in a blanket!

When they told her she had a girl they said that I was really small, and did not think I'd last the night. I was put in doll's clothes and christened two hours later at my mother's insistence. My mother said she knew that if I survived that night my grandmother would protect me as I had been born on her birthday, and she would be my guardian angel.

My mother was not told I was disabled until I came out of hospital five months later. She was also told, at that time, that I was totally blind. I began to see in one eye at the age of four. I remember seeing light, then shadows. It took six months for me to see properly in that eye. Being able to see frightened me. I wondered what was going on. Can you understand that?

They said to my mother that I would never walk BUT I DID! They said to me that I would never have children BUT I DID! I HAD TWO BOYS! They have children of their own now. Everything they said I would never do I DID!

So, you see, every day of my life is a bonus for me, and I am very grateful!

Leonard Cheshire

Peter Semper

I get a lot of fulfilment from
helping my wife at home.
She does not ask me to
help but I do it
spontaneously.
I can take out the
hoover if I feel like it.
It makes her happy
and I am also happy.
It comes naturally to
me because I used to
do a lot of things at home
for my mother, such as shopping, working in the
house etc. She also taught me to cook, iron, wash
clothes etc. so I am glad to be so self sufficient
today.

Leonard Cheshire

Peggy Priddle

I used to love to walk along
the beach and dream.
I walked with bare feet and
loved the feeling of the
water lapping around
my feet. I particularly
loved walking alone.
It was a meditation,
and troubles were made
much easier.

I can see myself as a young girl, wearing a cotton
flowery dress, with a frill round the bottom, and
short puffy sleeves. I wore a beret which was the
fashion at the time.

I think a lot about my past.

Leonard Cheshire
Ina Stephens

I think a smile is very important.

In the modern world people

seem to be so tied up in

their lives they often forget

to smile. They often bypass

people as they go about

their busy lives.

I feel much better when

someone smiles at me.

It can be any size and at

any time of day.

Leonard Cheshire

Dionne Neblett

In February, 2002, I went, with a

group from Randall Close, to the

Yvonne Arnaud Theatre in

Guildford to see the play

"A Woman of No Importance"

which I enjoyed. Because

of the title I presume it

was about a lady of whom

the men didn't think much.

After seeing the play I wanted to see it again when it

came to London but I didn't.

Leonard Cheshire

Jean Nicholls

I went for a stroll by the river.

It was so tranquil and peaceful.

We watched the boats go by.

What I think was the nicest

part of it was that there

were very few people.

It was nice to get away

from the hubbub of everyday

life. It was like being in

another world.

Leonard Cheshire
Reg Saunders

I enjoyed the afternoon when

Elizabeth Ceesay did "Desert Island

Music in Mind." I had to

concentrate on what Elizabeth

was trying to say. For a while,

I was unaware of recent loss,

and the problems facing me at the moment.

Editors' Note: 'Music in Mind' is a regular music session in Randall Close.
We believe that good music has the power to heal, inspire, and unite us all.

Leonard Cheshire

John Garland

My philosophy of life is to

help other people if I can.

That makes me feel good.

Another thing I love is

when I hear a baby

say its first words.

I saw my first opera,

"Aida", at the age of

seven, when I went with

my father to Sadler's Wells.

I have been passionate about opera ever since.

My favourite is "La Bohème.

Leonard Cheshire

Writer Anon.

The thrill

of

learning

a new

skill

Leonard Cheshire
Pam Swaine

I felt great joy recently when

my son and I were on our

own and we just talked

and talked about

everything. It was heaven.

It really was.

Talking with someone very dear is so

special because we rarely get the chance.

Julie Walker

MY MOST JOYOUS MOMENT

Going to Egypt

Standing in the Valley of
the Kings and Queens
I became quite emotional
at treading the same
footsteps as dynasties,
and witnessing
architecture from a
previous millennium.
The sense of spirituality
and romance brought tears
to my eyes and a lump
in my throat.

Truly a moment to be thankful for.

Leonard Cheshire

Bipin Samant

I enjoy coming to Randall Close

on the days when I have

holistic treatment such as

massage, relaxation and

breathing exercises.

My awareness is

heightened and I feel

more relaxed and happy.

What a pity everyone can't

experience this!

Leonard Cheshire

Writer Anon.

Good health, lots of money,

at least enough to live

well, and a good, rich

man is all I need!

Those are the

basics. Everything

else comes after that!

I love my oysters and champagne as often as

possible!

Leonard Cheshire
Maria Lewis

I love my grandchildren. I love my family. I am very happy when they come to see me, especially when my son comes. I feel lit up in their presence. When they are not with me I think of them and feel better. I do not feel disabled when they are with me.

Thank God I have my brother-in-law to help me!

My older sister is a very good person. She visits me every afternoon, helps me walk along my corridor, and we talk about the 'old days' and always have a good laugh.
My younger sister visits me every week and brings me cake. I love it!

I love my granddaughter Maria Louisa to whom I can tell anything and with whom I feel very comfortable and at ease.
I feel spiritually uplifted when Francesca, my granddaughter, is around. In fact, I absolutely adore all my grandchildren!

Sometimes, when I am feeling low, I clutch the beautiful hand-made card my son gave me thirty years ago. When I hold it I can feel his love and goodness and I feel better. Also, I love my daughter very much, and her wonderful caring ways have helped me so much on life's path.

cont'd.

Leonard Cheshire

I remember going home to my parents in Greece and seeing "WELCOME HOME' in big colourful letters on a banner hanging over the gate. What a lovely thought! I had a very happy childhood in Greece.

I remember, when I was young, I used to go swimming a lot as we lived by the sea. One day I was wearing a completely new outfit. I saw an elderly neighbour in the water as if he was falling backwards. I forgot about the new outfit, which I loved, and I dived in and saved him. I managed to balance him, and when I came out, I saw my outfit, totally spoiled. As I discuss this contribution, thoughts of that day come flooding back, and I am laughing!

However, I also remember great sadness because, when the Germans occupied Greece, he disappeared with all the other Jews and I never saw him again. When I grew up I realised why!

Jhotsna Poojara

I am a Hindu. When life becomes
difficult I always pray to God.
Prayer helps me see my way
and work things out. All my
life I have gained peace
through prayer, as a child in
India, then in East Africa
where I had my children,
and in London where
I came in 1964.

Prayer has helped me through all the changes
and difficulties.

Thank goodness I have had God to help me!

Writer Anon.

The

heightened

awareness

of meditation.

Veronica Patricia Thomas

BEING DISABLED

Being disabled means that there are certain tasks you cannot undertake - be aware of this but don't give up because being disabled is not the end of the world, or the end of your life. It sometimes makes us very negative beings, but we have to try and overcome this.

I know there are varying degrees of disability, but provided we still have our faculties, we should strive to remain positive and to always stimulate and utilise the brain as much as we possibly can. Not every disabled person can do this, especially the severely disabled, but there are other options for them.

We must remain a part of society, and it is therefore important that we demonstrate this for all the non-believers out there, but first and foremost do this for ourselves. This is a booster for our self-esteem and will motivate us to try and undertake other tasks which are well within our reach.

I believe that being positive will draw positive energies toward us. We have enough to contend with - we do not need negative energies.

Leonard Cheshire

GO OUT THERE and enroll in a college. Do some volunteer work. Become an active member of society. When I became disabled, I decided not to sit around and wallow in self-pity. Instead, I decided to put some, if not all of my energy, into painting etc.

MOTIVATE yourselves. You may ask what makes me so positive - well, I tell myself there are people out there with more disabilities than I.

FOOD FOR THOUGHT...

Veronica Patricia Thomas

RELAXATION

Relaxation can have the most desired effect on the human body. After a session of deep relaxation our awareness is heightened and, therefore, we are able to deal sensibly with any given situation.

PAIN

Relaxation can help to alleviate pain to a certain degree. I am sure we are all aware that tension increases pain. Relaxation is not a cure for pain(if you have extreme pain, always seek medical advice), but it will aid in the release of tension and the subsidence of pain to a certain degree. When the body is in pain, we automatically tense that part which is affected.

STRESS

Relaxation is good for stress because it comes from deep within. Every cell in the body notices the relaxation that is being given. It is harmonious development of body, mind and spirit. In relaxation, spiritual awareness is essential. Relaxation is good for personal development.

Create the right atmosphere, ignite some candles, burn some essential oils, and make yourself comfortable. Begin by breathing deeply from the diaphragm. Choose a room where you will not be disturbed.

ENJOY!

Leonard Cheshire
Winefride E. Lowe

I remember vividly the first time

I went to Holy Communion.

I was in uniform, Auxiliary

Territorial Service. It was

in a small, rather plain,

little Church which

had an extraordinary,

prayerful atmosphere.

When I think about it I am still there. It was

December 1944.

Leonard Cheshire
Winefride E. Lowe

To me, one of the most joyful and creative times in my life is when I write a poem which is truthful to me, and which I consider to be reasonably good. I always feel in better health after I have finished a poem.

Here is one of mine:-

NIGHT HARVEST
I should be sleeping, gathering from God
Love, strength and wisdom for the coming day,
But this previous darkness enlivens me.
No moon, but I see white stars
And I am humbled, then lifted with joy.
Sheen of frost on grass, small leaves lightly moving,
Tall fir tree, silver tipped and menacing.
Stubby fence with sharp, iced spikes,
Almost leafless elder, displaying silvered wands,
The common nettle, now like a dancer
Weaving a fine, white, silver-touched veil,
And enhancing all, the awesome God-in-Control mystery
Of the splashing, hissing sea, unseen but near.
Sleep? At a time like this?
I will sleep when my body must.

cont'd.

Leonard Cheshire

Now, I fill my heart seeing so much beauty within
darkness.
When dawn strokes the welcoming dull green sea
I will give thanks for the outpouring of golden fire.
This moment, the night has glints of transparent silver,
And these I gather, my spiritual treasures,
Which, soundless, shapeless, and limitless,
Spin a shimmer and shine before my eyes
Like compassionate whispers, darts of love,
Blessings, disguised for earthly eyes to see.

A Poem written by
Winefride E. Lowe 2002

Leonard Cheshire

Winefride E. Lowe

Most "classical" music

is a treasure to me.

Three cheers for

Beethoven!

He would save

my sanity on

a desert island!

Leonard Cheshire

Winefride E. Lowe

A good book has pulled

me out of many a

difficult situation.

Reading a well

written book

on a worthwhile

subject clears my

mind and helps me to

solve problems.

Leonard Cheshire
Helen Ruzic

I first started to do yoga when I came to the day centre in 1996 and met the yoga teacher. She has taught me in the pink room for the six years I have been coming to the centre. She also has yoga groups where we can talk about things that are special to us.
Yoga also makes you think and teaches you to take deep breaths.

There is also a lady who gives massage in the pink room to people who have back problems and find it hard to move around. She loosens the muscles in their backs and shoulders which is very nice and it also does you good. I have been going to her for the past six years and enjoyed every minute of it.

The effect the pink room has on me is one that is so calming. If I am in a bad mood it goes immediately. It doesn't matter who I am with, the pink room is the best room in the place.

Leonard Cheshire
Ricky Lowe

If (WHEN) I get really LOW, or depressed, I try any of the following:-

1. Listening to a quality piece of serious music, Duke Ellington Orchestra, Ella Fitzgerald, Louis Armstrong, Eric Clapton, Fleetwood Mac (old & new), Horselips, or any of the 100+ groups, singers, orchestras.

2. Looking at a favourite piece of GREAT ART by a Great Artist - (usually famous) - Matisse, Raphael, Emile Knolde and many, many others.

3. Reading a really good piece of 'transporting' prose that can take one to another world with its 'word pictures', and maybe teach or re-enforce some wisdom (examples Sir Ernest Gowers - Essays, and most of the best 10% of literature, all kinds).

4. Reading ANY GREAT poem, whether a favourite or not, as this to me is 'travel in the mind' to another place, state of being, emotion, aesthetic state.

5. Creating a piece of artwork, or poetry , or music.

ALL the above CAN help me cheer up.

Leonard Cheshire
Val Vallentyne

I think travel broadens the mind. If the world had no boundaries probably there would be no wars.

I thoroughly enjoyed every country I visited, which I did when we were in the army.

My husband's previous service was in the navy. That was towards the end of the war in the Far East under Lord Mountbatten.

One of my joys in life has been seeing my children grow through travel. I wanted them to get to know other cultures and languages and their friends were always welcome in our home.

It was tough at times but, looking back, the knowledge and interest of it all was so rewarding. I remember it fondly.

The first country we visited was Cyprus which took three weeks to get to in those days by boat. On the way, we visited Malta, Gibraltar, and Egypt where we stayed in transit for one month. That gave us the opportunity to go up and down the Nile and visit the Suez Canal.

We saw a lot of Cyprus while there.

Our next posting was back to England, in Colchester. Then, we were off for six years to many different parts of Germany, before returning to Colchester.

On leaving the military, we remained in Colchester before eventually going to work in London.

Thinking about all this today is just like it was yesterday!

I did not stop my travelling. I continued to visit many parts of Europe.

Leonard Cheshire

Royce Miller

I started stargazing as a very young
man. Of course, today it is known
better as astronomy.

When I came out of the army
I began to take an interest
in the sky, the universe,
and U.F.O.s. All my life
I have been fascinated by
this. In fact, I have two
telescopes. I made one
myself. The other
is American.

I feel happy when I take
out my telescope and look
at the night sky.

I'd like to have been able to go to all those places I
have been looking at all my life.

Leonard Cheshire
Cyrenius McCurbin

I am a calypso man.

As a Jamaican

I love reggae

and calypso.

It cheers me

up and I feel

better. I think the

right music also

helps my health.

Leonard Cheshire
Sue Groves

The best joy of my life was

when both my children

were back together again.

To be a whole family

means so much to

me. It gives me

pride and joy to see

them grow up together.

Leonard Cheshire
Ernest Hale

My life moved into another
dimension when I became
a grandfather. Although
I sometimes feel my years,
when they are around
I am 'live and kicking!'

They make life
worthwhile and give
me reason to go on.
It's so nice to see
them creating things
and enjoying life.

I think a tightly knitted family can get over
many of life's problems.

Leonard Cheshire
Ellen Ralph

I thoroughly enjoyed the

special "Music in Mind"

when it was Peggy Priddle's

"Desert Island Discs."

It was a lovely afternoon.

The music was really nice and sentimental,

and I liked Peggy's choice.

NB: See also note
on page 39

The Late Joan Hubbert

THE PARK.......

To me conjures up space, greenery, light,

hustle and bustle of everyday life.

People, animals, trees, bright flowers, peace.

A profusion of extremes, of buildings - there were aplenty.

The Millennium Gallery, The Coffee Shop, where poets

and others merge to participate in a common interest.

Poetry - to listen, to recite, to discuss, act out.

With beauty all around.

The splish-splash of the water.

Tranquillity.

These are but a few of

Battersea Park's wider spectrum.

A Poem written by
Joan Hubbert 2002

Leonard Cheshire
Elizabeth Ceesay

Ever since I did "Desert Island Music In Mind" it is as if I am free. I feel as if something happened that day. I feel truly a woman now. My mind was so full of remembrances. It was wonderful to go back.

My Scottish schoolteacher in The Gambia had so much influence on me.

I am so grateful to have been given this opportunity to hear the Scottish music I so love. It was made possible for me to relive the magic of my childhood in Africa.

I always used to say that I am Black Scottish! Scottish music always uplifts me.

I will never forget that day for as long as I live!

NB: See also note on page 39

Leonard Cheshire

Elizabeth Grant

As soon as I saw the view from the corridor through the pink room I felt satisfied and so relaxed. The door was open to the outside and I had stopped to look. The sun was shining on the tree outside, and the atmosphere made me feel so relaxed and satisfied. The light shone and everything was just blooming.

I stopped in my tracks. As I saw the beauty it attracted my attention and I had to say something. It was just wonderful!

Sometimes you see something that suddenly lifts your spirits up. We don't need money all the time! Something like this can make you feel happy too.
You just have to look!

Leonard Cheshire

Writer Anon.

Allowing the

music of

Beethoven

to waft

over me

while relaxing

on the floor.

Leonard Cheshire
Misha Hazelwood

I like listening to music with my eyes
shut and just listening to the
different sounds. I like different
music for my different moods
and times in my life.

I don't have a favourite type.
I feel it is very personal.

It can have a variety of
sounds. In fact, you can be
anywhere and you don't
have to have a radio.

Just close your eyes and switch off from everything
around you.

Leonard Cheshire
Vivian Spanton

THINGS THAT GIVE ME PLEASURE

1. Having always been a ridiculously early riser, I love to sit and watch the sunrise. The break of dawn instigating the tuning of the 'dawn chorus' as the birds awake.

2. The Summer, when I can have my patio door open and watch, what I call, my urban nature. Watching the squirrels hop skipping and jumping around the garden.

3. The gurgling, hiccoughing laugh of small babies when you tickle them.

4. The faces of children at Christmas as they open their presents.

5. The sound of people at a party, enjoying themselves and making new friends.

6. The happiness when I see all my friends in Spain.

7. Spring flowers blooming, suggesting that Summer is on the way.

8. The look of sheer joy on my mother and husband Ray's faces as I took my first steps when I first became disabled.

Leonard Cheshire
Jeffrey Lindsay

I like reading for relaxation. It is
a way I can use my brain and
travel in my mind. I can go all
over the world without leaving
my chair. It is a good way to
exercise my brain.

Since becoming disabled
I now read much more,
and I have discovered
many different kinds
of books from the ones
I read before. I am learning
more about different things.

It's fun exploring things in life I have never
experienced before.

Leonard Cheshire

Peggy Cameron

I had not been to the theatre for

many years so it was wonderful

to go to a show with the Randall

Close group. I saw

"Phantom of the Opera"

which was so colourful,

and I liked all the

different kinds of music.

When I think about it now the memory makes me

feel happier.

Leonard Cheshire
Padmini De Almeida

1) To mingle with the innocent

   toddlers at play gives us immense

   pleasure! The arguments etc.

   are always so amusing.

2) Travelling and learning

   about other people's

   cultures. That stimulates

   me, and we can gather

   knowledge about diverse nationalities.

   Travelling definitely broadens our outlook on life.

Leonard Cheshire

Stephenson Joseph

I like being in company with people.
I like people in general, just so long as
I can get on with them. I hope they
get on with me too. Sometimes in
my life I do not feel that I am
equal with others because of my
disability. You see, I was a very
active person who loved sport.
I sometimes feel stagnant.

Nowadays, however, since
coming to Randall Close, I am
trying to get involved, and this is
helping me with these feelings.

I know I will feel a lot better if I can engage my mind
more. So, it will be good for me to join in with more of
the activities on offer, get to know more people, and
make some new friends.

Leonard Cheshire
Kusum Kanani

I like exercising and relaxing.

After I've done it I feel

much better. You feel so

relaxed and your mind

is easy. It is a lovely

feeling. I just close my

eyes and go along

with it.

I like to get away from the noise of life. There is

too much of it.

JUST SITTING IN WATER

It is all about water for me; it relaxes
me and eases the pain. Just sitting
in it, my body is more comfortable,
my mind is more relaxed, and
I get great enjoyment from
watching other people enjoying
themselves.

I especially love seeing my son
having fun. It is a way for him
not to worry about me.
He is having time for himself.
We used to do so many things
together, so now, this is very special,
as it is the only physical activity
we still share.

On our last family holiday we went on some boat cruises.
I found these equally relaxing, and the midnight one full
of magic and mystery.

Leonard Cheshire
Joan Arnold

My best way of relaxing is to do puzzles or crosswords. It makes me concentrate and then I do not have time to worry. It takes my mind off other things that might be troubling me.

Doing puzzles is definitely my way of relaxing.

I am elated and excited when I see something beautiful, especially scenery.

I love to look at rooftops and the various patterns they make against the sky. The scenery of mountains and villages in Europe is particularly beautiful, especially when the buildings are higgledy piggledy denoting many different periods of history. The sight of the rows of rooftops in these circumstances can be breathtaking. The texture and colour look almost alive, and they look as if they have just grown out of the earth.

It is history before my eyes. Rooftops tell us so much.

On the subject of texture, I love to go and look, and touch, beautiful materials, especially theatrical. It's so inspiring and food for the senses.

cont'd.

Leonard Cheshire

Even dried flowers can come alive. It makes you think and expands creativity. This all helps my artwork. All the memories come flooding back and build on each other. Even inanimate objects can have some effect if we **really look** with our minds instead of staring blankly at something.

Just look with your mind! There is so much beauty all around to fill your soul.

Leonard Cheshire
Margaret Blount

I love going to interesting places.

My number one is the

London Planetarium.

I loved watching

the moon and stars.

Looking up makes me

feel good.

I really, really like football! I am a big fan.

Leonard Cheshire
Writer Anon.

I had two strokes so where do I start?
Would you believe it, they were both on Christmas Eve,
one in 1975, the other in 1978? Funnily enough, on **both**
occasions, I was celebrating with friends, and drinking
champagne. I just collapsed in the middle of the parties!
Both times "they" thought I was just larking about and
that I had drunk too much. When "they" tried to
waken/revive me they couldn't get a peep out of me
because I was unconscious.

On **both** occasions ambulances were called and I was
rushed to hospital.

Both times, a blood clot was found hidden away
somewhere in the labyrinth of my brain.

After the operations, the doctors said, **both** times, that I
would never walk again, but, I proved them wrong on
both occasions! I was determined to walk again!

I was really really so determined to be on my feet. I just
never gave up, despite all the knocks and falls I had.
Today, I am still on my feet and living a full life.

Leonard Cheshire
William J. Gallagher

The older I become the more I realise the tremendous joy and inspiration my mother, Joan Gallagher, has been to me, and what a profound legacy she has left me.

I was a child in Ireland when I discovered this "Kind of Joy" through caring, first for my grandmother, and then for my mother.

During her short life, my mother showed me that I had an innate gift for empathy with other people, and gave me a deep sense of self worth and empowerment which I still have to this day.

Her example has stood me in good stead in my professional life, particularly since joining The Leonard Cheshire Foundation. Rosemarie Mitchell, who herself has spiritual wisdom, acknowledged this gift within me, and provided the opportunity where I could be in a position to influence more people.

It was at this point that my mother's legacy really came to fruition. Just as I had seen my mother do all those years ago, The Quality, The Dignity, Her Gift, through me, continues to enable and empower others.

What A Legacy!

cont'd

Leonard Cheshire

I have always found joy in the poetry of William Butler Yeats. This is one of my favourites which I dedicate to my father:-

He wishes for the Cloths of Heaven

Had I heavens' embroidered cloths,
Enwrought with golden silver light,
The blue and the dim and the dark cloths
Of night and light and the half - light,
I would spread the cloths under your feet:
But I, being poor, have only dreams;
I have spread my dreams under your feet;
Tread softly because you tread on my dreams.

See page 119

Leonard Cheshire

Writer Anon.

The first

view

of the sea

after

a long

journey.

Leonard Cheshire

Catherine Leppard

I like coming to Randall Close

and my pleasure is the

mosaic work I do,

also the pottery.

I look forward to

Tuesdays and I find

everyone so kind

and helpful.

I make a beeline for

the art room every week.

I just love it there, and

I feel really happy when

I leave for home.

Leonard Cheshire
Eric Jeffers

I used to work in The Royal British Legion Poppy Factory in Richmond, Surrey. I felt amazing achievement doing that work. It was very gratifying. I did it for fifteen years, working on my own when I worked on 3000 different badges each year. It was very intricate, concentrated work. The blades for all the fine work were very fine and you had to be really experienced to use them or else! Fingers could be very badly carved up!

There were around 650 different regiments and associations all requiring badges.

I was kept busy from one Armistice to the next!

It is uplifting for me to know that I was able to do that work, and I often think about it, especially on Armistice Day.

Every year the Queen Mother would come to place a cross on the tomb of the Unknown Soldier at Westminster Abbey. Every year I made that cross.

I met Her Majesty on a few occasions at the Garden of Remembrance.

I was also responsible for making the wooden cut-out of The Falkland Islands in 1982 which was then covered with poppies. Her Majesty The Queen came to see us that year and I have fond memories of her talking to me.

Leonard Cheshire

Karen Roberts

Why is the world crying?

There is more than enough

Love to go around, when

I consider how my two children

Have made me realise how easy it is

To give love.

A Poem written by
Karen Roberts 2002

Leonard Cheshire

Tom Rees

When I was a kid during the war I started making model aeroplanes out of anything I could lay my hands on. Everyone was really keen on aviation in those days. I lived in Deal then, and we could see the planes coming back from bombing Germany, and the white trail they left behind in the sky I shall never forget.

Of course, Group Captain Lord Cheshire V.C., O.M., D.S.O., D.F.C., who founded our organisation was a bomber pilot during the war.

Flying was a big deal in those days. Now it has become very pedestrianised.

I was passionate about getting all the details right. The intricacy of the work was a wonderful hobby, and I have carried it on all my life.

As life moved on we started to get better materials and more information about the planes. Prior to this, there was not much information available, so we had to do our best with what we had.

cont'd

Leonard Cheshire

Eventually, I was able to join Clubs and Associations and flew four times to competitions in Prague. The Czechoslovakians were very good and usually won the competitions. However, it was fascinating to talk to them about the war, and particularly the planes.

On one of my trips to America I took one of my models. That was just after I had been made redundant, and my wife and I made a special trip touring the country. We also were able to go to some model aeroplane competitions.

We also saw where General Custer took his last stand. On the memorial we were amazed to see the Irish name of someone who was probably a relative of my wife. The name was Geoghegan, and most of them had gone to America during the Irish Potato Famine.

So, model aeroplane making has been a joy and passion for me all my life, and I still am able to do a little today, despite my disability.

Leonard Cheshire
Paul Clissold

In the eighteen months

I have worked here at

Randall Close the

most pleasure

has been watching

people blossom as

they have learnt new skills.

Thank you.

THE NOSE HAS IT!

Oh how I adore aromas - well most anyway! The sheer joy, pleasure and uplift the sense of smell gives me transcends words.
I just give a thousand thanks each day for its presence. It is a true life enhancer. There is an abundance of aromas. So, here are a few to set your noses twitching! :-

Early morning mountain air through all the seasons.

A summer bonfire.

Woodland - conifer in summer and deciduous during autumn.

The sea or ocean.

A baby's skin, especially the back of the neck.

A lover, particularly their pillow!..

Freshly cut grass and hay - fortunately allergy free zones for me!

Fresh coffee and baking bread.

Jhotsna Poojara, Kusum Kanani, or Waverney Lewis's cooking has me 'jumping for joy' !

Leonard Cheshire

Paul Martin

I love to play

tennis, especially

on a hot day,

then have

a shower,

and relax

and sunbathe.

Bliss!

Leonard Cheshire

Chi Chi Okonkwo

When you choose

to respond to

life's difficulties

with compassion

and love,

instead of fear

and doubt, you

create a "heaven

on earth."

Leonard Cheshire

Writer Anon.

My mother always

said to "look for

people with good

character in life."

I have always

tried to do that.

Frank Colley

BALANCE AND HARMONY

Everyday in every way
I become more peaceful
and harmonious.
I accept other people as
they are without
expectations.
I handle my
responsibilities
with harmonious ease.
Negativity flows
through me without
affecting me.
I peacefully accept the
things I cannot change, and change the things I
can. I am at peace with myself, the world, and
everyone in it.

Balance and Harmony are my key words for

condition response.

I detach from worldly pressures and retreat to

calm inner space.

Leonard Cheshire
Frank Colley

TRUE FRIENDSHIP

The proper way to create friends is

through a warm heart and not simply

money or power. Friends of power, and

friends of money, are something different.

They are usually not friends.

Leonard Cheshire

Writer Anon.

The glow you

feel when

receiving a

beautifully

wrapped

present.

Vanessa Court

WHAT MAKES ME FEEL JOY

* Riding on my bike through the
   traffic with the wind in my hair,
   while all others are in cars
   waiting in queues.

* Digging in my garden,
   planting plants, watching
   flowers grow.

* Sitting wrapped up on my
   sofa on a cold winters night
   with my hot water bottle
   and a movie.

* My cats.

* Nice food.

* My lovely husband.

Catherine Alison Fisher

What brings me the most joy?
There are so many of them.
But, there are the special ones
such as, the happiness
of friends who involve
you in their life.

The closeness of family
when you can share
experiences with them.

Also, the little things that make up a day, you
hardly notice them. The sounds of life, the vision of
sun sparkling on the river Thames, someone
walking past you laughing with a friend.

Laughter in general lightens me up inside.

Leonard Cheshire

Georgette Tra

When I lost my brother recently

I cried and cried. We were so

close and I loved him

so much. I still feel he is

around me every day

so he is not gone from

my life. I will never

forget him.

His daughter is only five years old and I will

always do everything I can to help her. Soon, I

will go to West Africa to see her, and I will always

love her the way I loved my brother. She is his

blood.

Geraldine Barrett

Since I have been coming to the Day Centre, which has been about five years now, there has been a good improvement in myself.

With my yoga meditation group, which I enjoy enormously, it gets down inside my body, and I feel good relief in my whole self.

I also feel good when I have massage. It seems to have a healing effect on my condition.

When I have setbacks with my illness quietness is very important to me. I always turn to what I have been learning at the Day Centre and that helps pull me through, even when I am at home.

I am learning more about myself. I am a fighter and do not let things keep me down for too long.

Before I started yoga I did not realise meditation was a part of it. Also, the breathing exercises are very important, especially when done with the stretches.

I'll keep on trying as long as I get good encouragement from my tutors in Randall Close.

Leonard Cheshire

Brizilla Malcolm

My greatest

enjoyment in

life,

and this

is the truth,

is being

able to serve the Lord.

Leonard Cheshire
Peter Glenday

I worked in a 4 star hotel in Durban, Natal, South Africa.
Lots of exciting things happened, also many amusing
things.

Once, I found one of the night managers behind the
counter blind drunk!

Another time, I found a night manager trying to nick the
hotel's money!

Many famous people passed through. Once I got the
autograph of Chief Buthelezi from Natal Province.

Another time, I met Barbara Windsor who also gave me
her autograph, also Terry Scott and June Whitfield.

When I think back I get a lot of pleasure from my
remembrances.

I will never forget the weight of my morning suit, and my
dinner jacket, which we had to wear every day as part of
our uniform. Can you imagine how hot that was in South
African temperatures? The air conditioning hardly worked
at all.

It was an interesting time in my life. I feel joy when I
remember those times in the 1960's and 1970's.

Leonard Cheshire

Doris Hood

I have a budgie called Jimmy. I let him fly about most of the time. He is great company and stops me from being lonely. You have to see him to believe it! He gets everywhere! I can't even read the paper in peace unless he is in his cage! When he is in the cage resting then I have time for myself. I teach him to speak which is a challenge for me.

I like television soaps. They also stop me from being lonely as I get involved in all their lives. Some people criticise television but, for someone like me, it is a lifeline.

There is always something which can bring joy into our lives.

The Late Albert Bearham

I read everyday. I am a big reader and
sometimes read a book a day.
I think I have covered the
world in books. I get a lot of
joy from reading.

I can remember a time when
we were young, five or six
of us would be gathered
around the warm coal fire
reading books. No one dared
interrupt another!
There was not a sound!

Books teach us so much,
including how to imagine.
There were books everywhere.

Sometimes I put myself in to the book I am reading, and
imagine I am there, wherever the plot is taking place.

I am there with it! You can really lose yourself!

Indira Valaydon Pillay

I have weekly massage in
hospital and have had for
the past year. Now, I am
also able to have it in
Randall Close which is
wonderful. Also, I have
relaxation here, and feel
more relaxed afterwards
and a little bit more joy.

I know this all helps me to cope with my illness.

I am indeed fortunate to have experienced the joy of sharing my holistic interpretation of yoga, in so many varied situations, over a period of thirty five years. I knew from the very beginning that it would become an integral part of my life.

Aspects of this ancient philosophy, and spiritual discipline, are that its practice has the power to unlock the tremendous potential inside each and every human being, and that it can be modified to suit everyone, whatever their age and individual needs.

I find great joy in its existence which is continuously with me enchanting my life.

cont'd

Leonard Cheshire

This is an ancient sanskrit poem which brings me
joy every time I read it:-

Look well to this day
for it is life
the very best of life.
In its brief course lie all
the realities and truths of existence.
    the joy of growth
    the splendour of action
    the glory of power.
For yesterday is but a memory
and tomorrow is only a vision,
but today if well- lived makes
every yesterday a memory of happiness
and every tomorrow a vision of hope.
Look well therefore to this day.

Leonard Cheshire

Patrick Joe Lynch

I like to improve the look of houses
and have always had great joy
tiling, plastering, and woodwork.
In Randall Close I can still do
some woodwork. It's like a
hobby for me.

I have a bungalow at Seaford
in Sussex. There, I am still
able to do a bit of gardening.
That is also a joy for me.

I love to see the sea. I love my wife and
family.

Leonard Cheshire

Bill Fidler

One of the best exercises there is is walking and I try to walk whenever I feel like it.

Also, I go to the swimming baths now and again for a swim. This is also one of the best exercises and I also like to swim in the sea. The salt water is easier for swimming and floating. The secret of floating is keeping your head well back. It is a good thing to learn to float properly as it is marvellous restful relaxation.

I have always been fond of the sea. During the war, I served in the Royal Navy. I was a seaman gunner and diver so I got to know the sea as well as anybody.

After the war I became a Merchant Seaman.

During these times I learned to tie all different kinds of knots and occasionally, to this day, I still do knot tying which helps me relax. A reef knot gets tighter the more you pull it but, a granny's knot will come undone (a granny's knot is a reef knot done wrongly).

How would you make fresh water out of salt water or sea water? The answer is to boil the water and catch the steam in another pot. The resulting liquid is then fresh water.

You can see that the sea and water have played a major part in my life and I have, on the whole, enjoyed it. One thing I did not enjoy, however, was when the ship was turned on its side by gigantic waves, and I wondered whether I was ever going to get ashore. Even when we were bombed and sunk, I made it!

Leonard Cheshire
Edna Loughran

I get a lot of enjoyment from my ten grandchildren, nine boys and one girl, called Nikki, who is the apple of my eye. The eldest is sixteen and the youngest a year old. They all live reasonably close to me so I am kept involved with them. This keeps me on my toes. As soon as the eldest one comes in he says, "Do you want a cup of coffee Nan?" He then makes it for me. I feel cossetted and looked after.

I feel they keep me young and stop me feeling my age. I am lucky. If they can't see me they ring me every day.

I don't have to get lonely. Keep busy! It helps.

I also visit my friends two or three times a week. I am lucky I have an electric scooter so I can get about.

If I keep myself busy I do not get depressed and lonely.

You must not give in to illness, or disability. Be determined! I always try.

Leonard Cheshire
Rosemarie Mitchell

All three are different but I love them the same,
My heart skips a beat when I hear their name.

Every milestone they reach I remember each one,
And savour the moment long after it's gone.

The wonderful feeling of having them near,
To share in their laughter or wipe away a tear.

I feel their small hands when they hug me so tight,
Their tiny wet lips when they kiss me goodnight.

Although they're not mine, they feel part of me,
They're the best in the world it's plain to see.

The feeling of joy is simply divine
Each moment I spend with those grandchildren of mine!

A Poem written by
Rosemarie Mitchell 2002

Leonard Cheshire
Carol Pexton

I find the comments of my grandchildren inspiring. They are so innocent. I feel so close to them, and they are very caring about the fact that I have lost my leg. They would do anything to get me another one!

Recently, I experienced near death but it was not my time. However, the experience has made me realise that I am not afraid of death anymore.

Two days before I became really ill my first great-grandchild was born. When I was in hospital I remember my grand-daughter urging me to get well for him. I remember her saying, "Come on Nan I've carried him for nine months. You've got to get well to see him!"

Those words put me in fighting spirit! Also, all my other grandchildren needed me too.

I keep a diary, which is now enough for a book about things they have done and said. I get lots of joy from reading it back.

I really don't know what I would do without my husband and my children.

Leonard Cheshire

Pamela Pope

I love the music of Mario Lanza. He was so handsome, sexy, and had come to bed eyes, and sang so beautifully. He was not just a tenor. He was a crooner as well.

When I was in hospital I took Mario with me. In the ward they all loved him so it was no problem.

His music helps me cope with life, and I always try to think positively.

The music of Mario Lanza, I know, helps me with all my disabilities. I play his music and watch his films nearly every day.

In my house I have my Mario Lanza room and that is my private joy!

Leonard Cheshire

Lucy Patterson

I love knitting,

and I love my children

and grandchildren.

What joy they give me!

Leonard Cheshire

Marion Frizzle

Love and understanding go hand in hand. It does not matter how much money you have. It can't buy love.

I am very fortunate. I've got a very good family. When I think of them I feel so happy. They ring me all the time and I am part of their lives. My husband is a very good man, one of the best. He really cares for me even though he is ill himself.

Sometimes I sit and cry, and sometimes I feel very down, but when I think of other people worse than I am, I feel better. I know I am very lucky!

If you have trust in God everything works out alright.

The Late Joan Hubbert

The colours of the rainbow...

Are made up of seven hues,

Red - orange - yellow - green -

Blue - Indigo, violet too,

These are the colours I associate with You.

Red is for the warmth you show creatures great and small,

Orange for the setting sun replacing skies of blue,

Yellow for the happiness you give to one and all,

Green is for the trees - your favourite colour too.

Blue is when I am feeling low,

Then I spend an hour with you,

Indigo is how I feel when that time is through,

BUT - violet is the best of all,

As it leaves a soft, warm glow,

When we part at the end of another day,

That I have spent with you.

A Poem written by
Joan Hubbert 2002

Permission Acknowledgement
The Leonard Cheshire Foundation, William J. Gallagher, and The Authors, gratefully acknowledge the permission of A. P. Watt Ltd. on behalf of Michael B. Yeats, to include in this anthology the poem, "He wishes for the Cloths of Heaven" by William Butler Yeats. This was taken from W. B. Yeats "The Love Poems" edited and annotated by A. Norman Jeffares published by Kyle Cathie Limited.